Stuck at Home with Jokes Malone

INTRO TO PHASE 5

/o_e/

Level 4+
Blue+

Helpful Hints for Reading at Home

The graphemes (written letters) and phonemes (units of sound) used throughout this series are aligned with Letters and Sounds. This offers a consistent approach to learning whether reading at home or in the classroom.

THIS BLUE+ BOOK BAND SERVES AS AN INTRODUCTION TO PHASE 5. EACH BOOK IN THIS BAND USES ALL PHONEMES LEARNED UP TO PHASE 4, WHILE INTRODUCING ONE PHASE 5 PHONEME. HERE IS A LIST OF PHONEMES FOR THIS PHASE, WITH THE NEW PHASE 5 PHONEME. AN EXAMPLE OF THE PRONUNCIATION CAN BE FOUND IN BRACKETS.

Phase 3			
j (jug)	v (van)	w (wet)	x (fox)
y (yellow)	z (zoo)	zz (buzz)	qu (quick)
ch (chip)	sh (shop)	th (thin/then)	ng (ring)
ai (rain)	ee (feet)	igh (night)	oa (boat)
oo (boot/look)	ar (farm)	or (for)	ur (hurt)
ow (cow)	oi (coin)	ear (dear)	air (fair)
ure (sure)	er (corner)		

New Phase 5 Phoneme	o_e (home, froze, slope)

HERE ARE SOME WORDS WHICH YOUR CHILD MAY FIND TRICKY.

Phase 4 Tricky Words			
said	were	have	there
like	little	so	one
do	when	some	out
come	what		

TOP TIPS FOR HELPING YOUR CHILD TO READ:

• Allow children time to break down unfamiliar words into units of sound and then encourage children to string these sounds together to create the word.

• Encourage your child to point out any focus phonics when they are used.

• Read through the book more than once to grow confidence.

• Ask simple questions about the text to assess understanding.

• Encourage children to use illustrations as prompts.

INTRO TO PHASE 5 /o_e/

This book introduces the phoneme /o_e/ and is a Blue+ Level 4+ book band.

Stuck at Home with Jokes Malone

Written by
John Wood

Illustrated by
Chloe Jago

Kid King sat in his home of stone.
His home was on a slope.

Kid King was not alone in his home.
His clown, Jokes Malone, was there too.

It was Kid King's job to help those in the town down the road.

For years and years there had been a thick frost. It was a long winter.

When Kid King woke up in the mornings, he spoke to those in the town.

"The ponds froze so we cannot go fishing," they said. "The fishing nets are no good."

"We have no food left," they said.
They had lost all hope.

Kid King had lots of food, but it was stuck with him in his stone home.

"Kick my bum," said Jokes Malone.
"That will be fun!"
But Kid King was too glum.

"Not now," said Kid King. "I need to get food to the town!"

Kid King chose a drone to lift the food into the town.

But as it went higher, the drone froze.
It fell back down and broke.

Kid King got a remote and drove a car with food in it.

But the car went into a skid. It broke as it hit a tree.

Kid King hung the food on rockets.
The rockets rose higher and higher.

But then the rockets began to explode.
The food fell back down like rain.

"Honk my nose," said Jokes Malone.
"That will be fun!"
But Kid King was too glum.

Jokes Malone got a balloon dog for fun.
"That is it!" said Kid King. "Balloons!"

Kid King stuck lots and lots of balloons to the throne.

Soon, the throne rose up into the air!
Kid King took the food and got on.

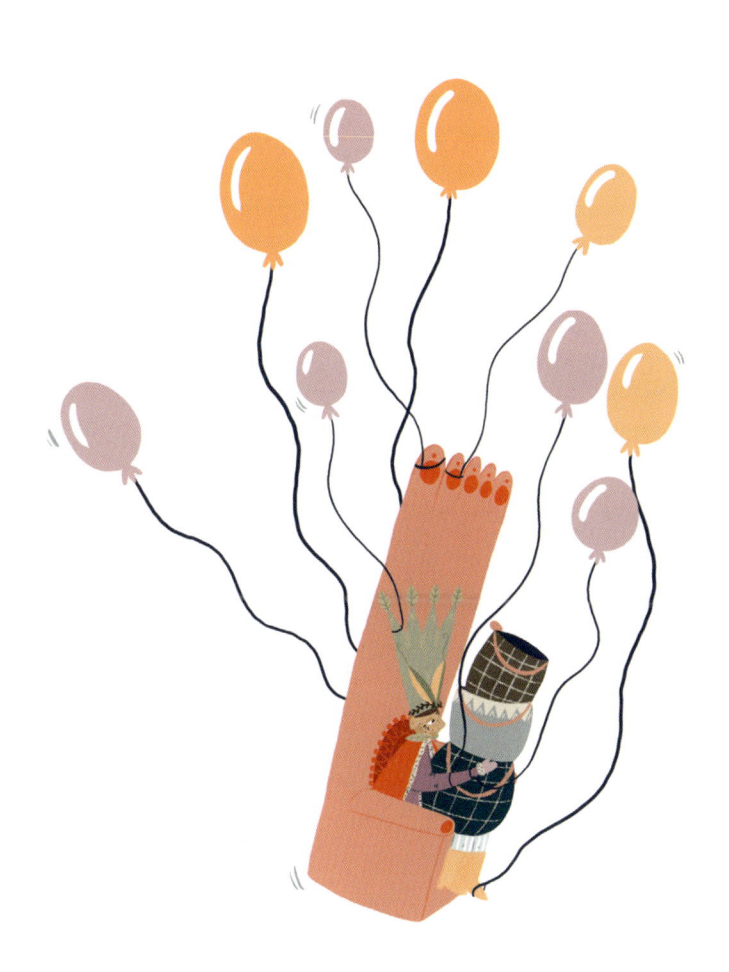

Kid King was high up. Look! There was the town. Smoke rose from the huts.

Kid King cut the ropes that held the balloons. The throne fell like a stone.

There was a yelp of fright from Kid King. "This will hurt!" he said.

But the throne fell on the fishing nets.
Kid King poked himself. He was not hurt!

"Come out," Kid King said. "I have dinner for all of you!"

"Wait for me!"
It was Jokes Malone. Now they were all there.

Stuck at Home with Jokes Malone

1) Who does Kid King live with?

2) Why did the town run out of food?

3) What was the first way Kid King tried to get food to the town?
   a) On a drone
   b) On a boat
   c) On a grumpy cat

4) How would you get food to the villagers? Would you invent something new?

5) Do you think it was right for Kid King to share his food? Why?

©2022 **BookLife Publishing Ltd.**
King's Lynn, Norfolk PE30 4LS

ISBN 978-1-80155-065-9

All rights reserved. Printed in Poland.
A catalogue record for this book is available from the British Library.

Stuck at Home with Jokes Malone
Written by John Wood
Illustrated by Chloe Jago

An Introduction to BookLife Readers...

Our Readers have been specifically created in line with the London Institute of Education's approach to book banding and are phonetically decodable and ordered to support each phase of the Letters and Sounds document.

Each book has been created to provide the best possible reading and learning experience. Our aim is to share our love of books with children, providing both emerging readers and prolific page-turners with beautiful books that are guaranteed to provoke interest and learning, regardless of ability.

BOOK BAND GRADED using the Institute of Education's approach to levelling.

PHONETICALLY DECODABLE supporting each phase of Letters and Sounds.

EXERCISES AND QUESTIONS to offer reinforcement and to ascertain comprehension.

BEAUTIFULLY ILLUSTRATED to inspire and provoke engagement, providing a variety of styles for the reader to enjoy whilst reading through the series.

AUTHOR INSIGHT:
JOHN WOOD

An incredibly creative and talented author, John Wood has written about 60 books for BookLife Publishing. Born in Warwickshire, he graduated with a BA in English Literature and English Language from De Montfort University. During his studies, he learned about literature, styles of language, linguistic relativism, and psycholinguistics, which is the study of the effects of language on the brain. Thanks to his learnings, John successfully uses words that captivate and resonate with children and that will be sure to make them retain information. His stories are entertaining, memorable, and extremely fun to read.

INTRO TO PHASE 5 /o_e/

This book introduces the phoneme /o_e/ and is a Blue+ Level 4+ book band.